This little pig went to market

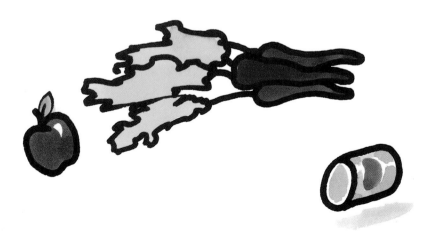

Oh where, oh where has my little dog gone?

Goosey goosey gander

4 & 20 blackbirds baked in a pie

Hickey pickey, my black hen

Little poll parrot sat in his garret

Hey diddle, diddle! The cat and the fiddle

Hickory dickory dock the mouse ran up the clock

The cow jumped over the moon

Now I lay me down to sleep